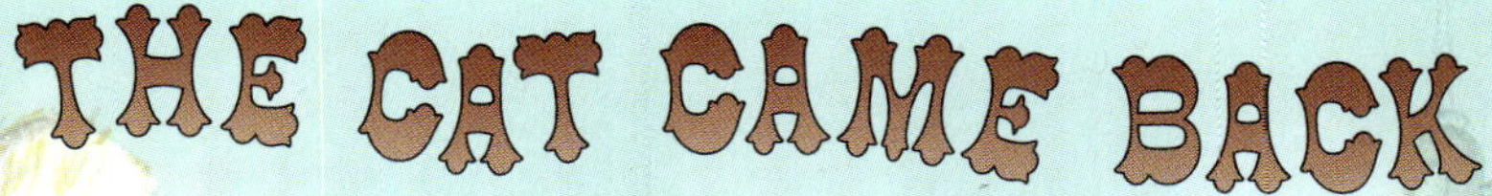

THE CAT CAME BACK

A Traditional Song
Illustrated by John Sandford

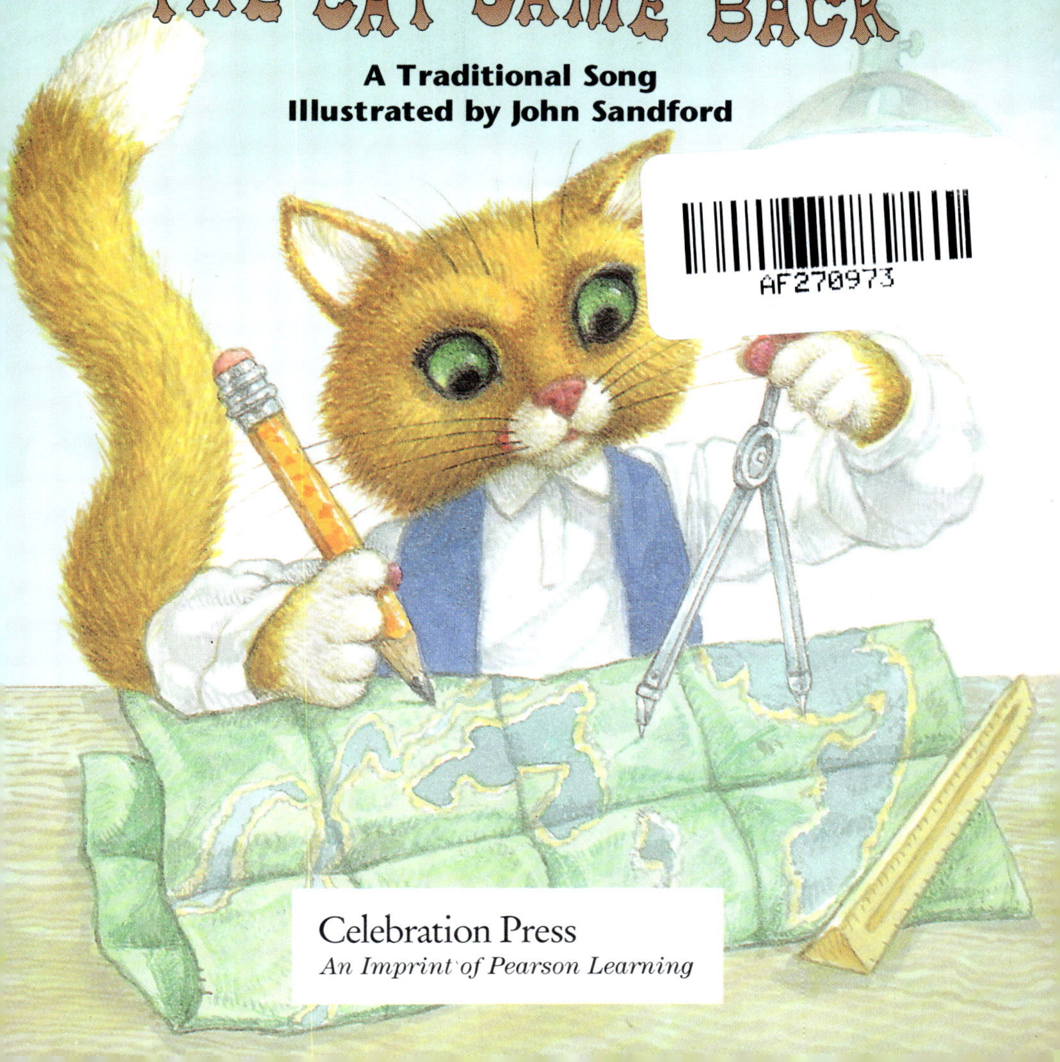

Celebration Press
An Imprint of Pearson Learning

Old Mister Johnson
had troubles of his own.
He had a yellow cat
that wouldn't leave his home.

He tried and he tried
to give the cat away.
He put it on a ship
going far, far away.

4

5

But the cat came back
the very next day.

The cat came back.
They thought he was a goner,
but the cat came back.
He just wouldn't stay away.

Mister Johnson gave the cat
to a man in a balloon.
He said, "Please take this cat
on a trip to the moon."

The balloon blew down
in a field far away.
Where the man is now,
well, no one wants to say.

But the cat came back
the very next day.

The cat came back.
They thought he was a goner,
but the cat came back.
He just wouldn't stay away.

Mister Johnson gave the cat
to a lady heading west.
He said, "The cat's a present
for the one you love the best."

13

The train hit a rock
and bounced along the rail.
Not a person could sit down
to tell this goofy tale.

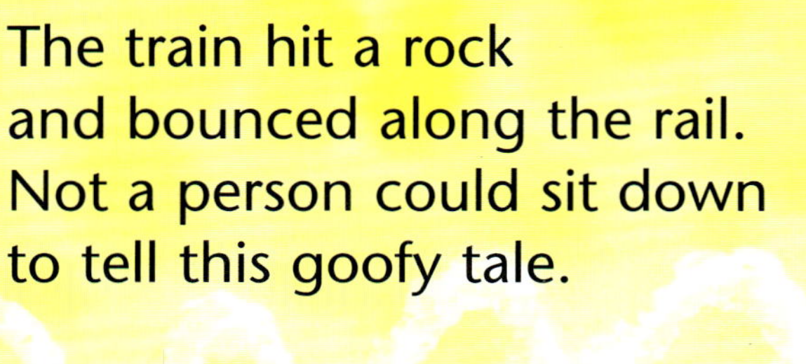

But the cat came back
the very next day.

The cat came back.
They thought he was a goner,
but the cat came back.
He just wouldn't stay away.

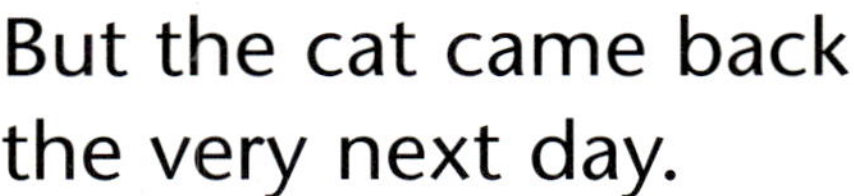

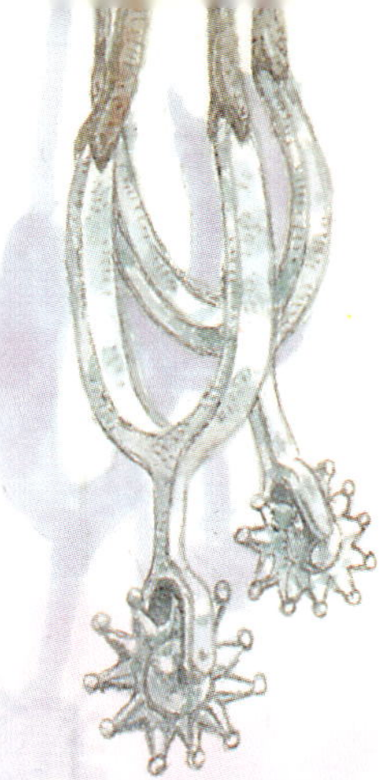